First Facts™

Everyday Character Education

Responsibility

by Kristin Thoennes Keller

Consultant:
Madonna Murphy, PhD, Professor of Education
University of St. Francis, Joliet, Illinois
Author, *Character Education in America's Blue Ribbon Schools*

Capstone
press

Mankato, Minnesota

First Facts is published by Capstone Press,
151 Good Counsel Drive, P.O. Box 669, Mankato, Minnesota 56002.
www.capstonepress.com

Library of Congress Cataloging-in-Publication Data
Thoennes Keller, Kristin.
  Responsibility / by Kristin Thoennes Keller.
  p. cm.—(First facts. Everyday character education)
  Includes bibliographical references and index.
  ISBN 0-7368-3683-7 (hardcover)
  1. Responsibility—Juvenile literature. I. Title. II. Series: First facts. Everyday character
education.
BJ1451.T49 2005
170—dc22   2004015502

Summary: Introduces responsibility through examples of everyday situations where this character
    trait can be used.

Editorial Credits

Amanda Doering, editor; Molly Nei, set designer; Kia Adams, book designer; Kelly Garvin,
    photo researcher

Photo Credits

Gem Photo Studio/Dan Delaney, cover, 5, 6–7, 9, 10–11, 12, 13, 19
Capstone Press/Karon Dubke, 1, 8
Corbis/Bettmann, 16–17
Kids Saving the Rainforest/Marianne Coates, 15
The Prudential Spirit of Community Initiative, 20

1 2 3 4 5 6 10 09 08 07 06 05

Table of Contents

Responsibility

Sam **promises** his parents he'll walk his younger sister home from school every day. Sometimes Sam's friends want him to stop and play. Sam walks his sister home first. Sam shows responsibility. He does what he says he will do.

Fact!
No one is born responsible. People learn to be responsible by doing their duties.

At Your School

Be responsible at school. Have your homework done every day. Following classroom rules shows responsibility. If a teacher gives you an extra job, do it quickly. Teachers trust responsible students to do special jobs at school.

With Your Friends

Responsible people are good friends.
Follow the family rules at a friend's
house. Take your shoes off by the door.

Responsible people keep their
promises. If you promise to play with
a friend, do it. Keep your plans, even if
you get an invitation from another friend.

At Home

Parents trust responsible children. Be responsible by doing your **chores** on time. You can help out by doing extra chores. Take responsibility for your own mistakes. Don't blame your mistake on your brother or sister.

Fact!
By being responsible, you can set a good example for your brothers and sisters.

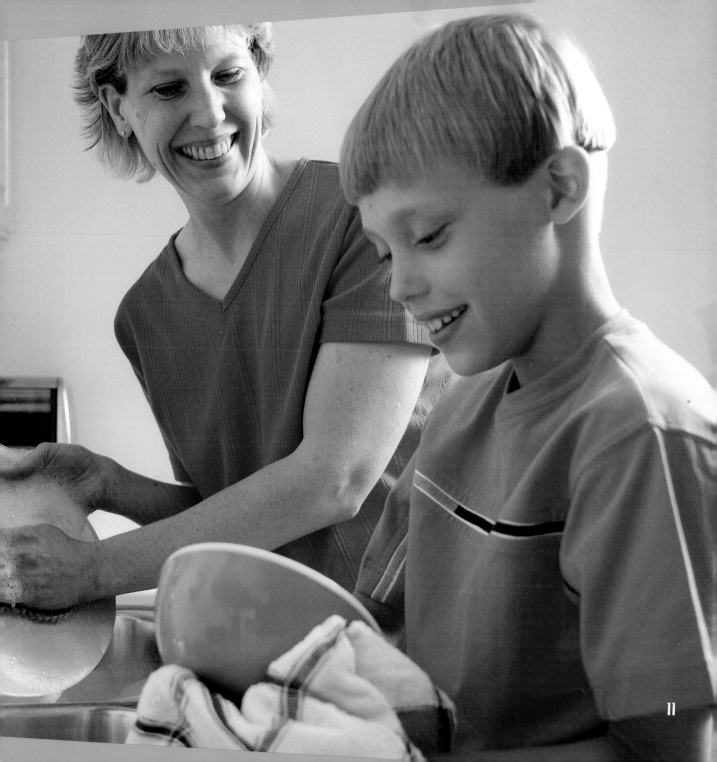

In Your Community

Responsible people take care of their **community**. Pick up after yourself and your pets. Put trash in the garbage can.

Responsible people care for others. **Volunteer** to help people in your community. You can give your used toys to children who need them.

Janine Licare-Andrews

Janine Licare-Andrews felt a responsibility to help the earth. At age 9, she and a friend started a group. They called it Kids Saving the Rainforest. The group helps plant trees and save animals in rain forests.

Fun Fact!

Janine and her friend earned money for their group by selling painted rocks on the side of the road.

Paul Revere

Paul Revere was a **patriot** soldier in the Revolutionary War (1775–1783). One night, Revere agreed to warn others that British enemies were coming. He rode his horse many miles in the dark to tell people. Revere showed responsibility by keeping his promise to warn others. He also took responsibility for the safety of others.

What Would You Do?

Sam agrees to walk the dog Saturday morning. That morning, Sam's friend Paulina asks him to play soccer. Sam wants to play right away. He could tie the dog to the fence and play soccer. What is the responsible thing for Sam to do?

Amazing but True!

When she was 14 years old, Sasha Bowers lived in a homeless shelter. While there, she formed a summer program for 250 other homeless children. With her help, the children were able to do fun activities. They planted a garden, went to museums, and fished. Sasha took responsibility for the younger children. She helped them have a good summer.

Hands On: Make a Chore Chart

Make a family chore chart so everyone knows who is responsible for certain chores around the house.

What You Need

white paper
marker
self-sticking notes

What You Do

1. Across the top of the paper, make three even columns and draw lines to the bottom of the chart.
2. Label the columns at the top of the paper with these words in this order: What? Who? Done!
3. In the What? column, write what jobs need to be done. Chores in your family might include setting the table, washing the dishes, or walking the dog.
4. Write the family members' names on the self-sticking notes. Stick the names in the "Who?" spaces to show who is responsible for that chore.
5. Each person can move their self-sticking note to the "Done!" column when finished with the chore.

Glossary

chore (CHOR)—a job that has to be done regularly; washing dishes and taking out the garbage are chores.

community (kuh-MYOO-nuh-tee)—a group of people who live in the same area.

patriot (PAY-tree-uht)—a person who sided with the colonies during the Revolutionary War

promise (PROM-iss)—to give your word you will do something

volunteer (vol-uhn-TEEHR)—to offer to do a job, usually without pay

Read More

Bender, Marie. *Responsibility Counts.* Character Counts. Edina, Minn.: Abdo, 2003.

Small, Mary. *Responsibility Is.* Character Education. Minneapolis: Picture Window Books, 2004.

Internet Sites

FactHound offers a safe, fun way to find Internet sites related to this book. All of the sites on FactHound have been researched by our staff.

Here's how:

1. Visit *www.facthound.com*
2. Type in this special code **0736836837** for age-appropriate sites. Or enter a search word related to this book for a more general search.
3. Click on the **Fetch It** button.

FactHound will fetch the best sites for you!

Index